DID YOU KNOW?

SPORTS

20 THINGS YOU DIDN'T KNOW ABOUT SOCCER

THEIA LAKE

PowerKiDS press.

Published in 2026 by The Rosen Publishing Group, Inc.
2544 Clinton Street, Buffalo, NY 14224

Portions of this work were originally authored by Ryan Nagelhout and published as *20 Fun Facts About Soccer*. All new material in this edition was authored by Theia Lake.

Editor: Greg Roza
Book Design: Tanya Dellaccio Keeney

Photo Credits: Cover PeopleImages.com - Yuri A/Shutterstock.com; p. 5 GIROMIN STUDIO/Shutterstock.com; p. 6 wutzkohphoto/Shutterstock.com; p. 7 Washington Imaging/Alamy Images; p. 8 https://upload.wikimedia.org/wikipedia/commons/2/21/One_Hundred_Children_in_the_Long_Spring.jpg; p. 9 Lordprice Collection/Alamy Images; p. 10 (left) charnsitr/Shutterstock.com; p. 10 (right) https://upload.wikimedia.org/wikipedia/commons/b/b7/1930_World_Cup_Final_Ball_Uruguay.jpg; p. 11 ACHPF/Shutterstock.com; p. 12 Bruce Leighty-Sports Images/Alamy Images; p. 13 Brent Clark/Alamy Images; p. 14 Ettore Griffoni/Shutterstock.com; p. 15 Cobalt S-Elinoi/Shutterstock.com; p. 16 kovop/Shutterstock.com; p. 17 ph.FAB/Shutterstock.com; p. 18 Xinhua/Alamy Images; p. 19 (Golden Boot) Marco Rubino/Shutterstock.com; p. 19 (Women's World Cup Trophy) Romain Biard/Shutterstock.com; p. 19 (British Premier League Trophy) Julian Prizont-Cado/Shutterstock.com; p. 19 (Olympic Gold Medal) fifg/Shutterstock.com; p. 19 (World Cup Trophy) Fitria Ramli/Shutterstock.com; p. 19 (Ballon D'Or) Fernando Astasio Avila/Shutterstock.com; p. 20 Ringo Chiu/Shutterstock.com; p. 21 Photo Works/Shutterstock.com; p. 22 Maxisport/Shutterstock.com; p. 23 IOIO IMAGES/Shutterstock.com; p. 24 https://upload.wikimedia.org/wikipedia/commons/4/42/Maradona_shilton_mano_dios.jpg; p. 25 (Ronaldo) Christian Bertrand/Alamy Images; p. 25 (Messi) Christian Bertrand/Shutterstock.com; p. 26 Gene Lower/Alamy Images; p. 27 Zuma Press, Inc/Alamy Images; p. 29 Photo 12/Alamy Images.

Cataloging-in-Publication Data

Names: Lake, Theia.
Title: 20 things you didn't know about soccer / Theia Lake.
Description: Buffalo, New York : PowerKids Press, 2026. | Series: Did you know? sports | Includes glossary and index.
Identifiers: ISBN 9781499450415 (pbk.) | ISBN 9781499450422 (library bound) | ISBN 9781499450439 (ebook)
Subjects: LCSH: Soccer–Juvenile literature.
Classification: LCC GV943.25 L35 2026 | DDC 796.334–dc23

Manufactured in the United States of America

CPSIA Compliance Information: Batch #CSPK26. For Further Information contact Rosen Publishing at 1-800-237-9932.

CONTENTS

WHAT'S FÚTBOL?

In the United States, many fans love to watch baseball and American football, two incredibly exciting sports with lots of history. However, soccer is the most popular sport in the world! There are soccer leagues all around the world, and national teams play in lots of different **tournaments**.

Outside of the United States, soccer is often called fútbol or football. No matter what you call it, it's a game that's just as fun to play as it is to watch!

There's so many fascinating facts about the historic game of soccer. Let' learn all about the world's most popular sport!

SOCCER SAYS

DID YOU KNOW?

Soccer terms are often very different from the terms used in other sports.

Most soccer terms come from England, where the sport's popularity grew rapidly. A soccer team is usually called a "club," and the names of many soccer teams include "FC," which stands for "football club." Soccer uniforms are called "kits." A soccer field is called the "pitch."

Football teams that have "united" in their name were often the result of two teams merging, or coming together, to make a new team.

Sunderland A.F.C. play their home games in the Stadium of Light in Sunderland, England. Their nickname is the Black Cats.

DID YOU KNOW?

The word "soccer" started as English slang for "football."

In England, soccer is often called "**association** football" because rugby was often called "rugby football." The sports were called "football" because they're played on foot, not on horseback like polo. The word "association" was often shortened to "assoc." Eventually this became the slang term "soccer."

A LONG TIME AGO...

DID YOU KNOW?

Games similar to soccer have been played all over the world for hundreds of years.

The Football Association was formed in England in 1863, but other games similar to soccer were played elsewhere years before. Perhaps the earliest form of soccer was played in China during the Han Dynasty (206 BCE–CE 220). Called tsu chu, it featured players kicking a ball filled with feathers!

This painting from the Song Dynasty, painted in the mid-1100s, shows children playing tsu chu, also called cuju. "Tsu chu" comes from the Chinese words for "kick" and "ball."

DID YOU KNOW?

Association football is hugely popular in England, but the sport has had its ups and downs.

For hundreds of years in England, soccer was banned on Sundays due to laws of the Church of England.

The Lord Mayor of London banned soccer in 1314 because of the trouble the games caused in the city. During the Hundred Years' War (1337–1453), the king banned soccer because he wanted people to practice military skills instead, such as archery.

ON THE PITCH

DID YOU KNOW?

Early soccer balls were made from... pig parts?

Not just any parts, pig **bladders**! Each ball would be a different size and shape, depending on the bladder. The first rubber soccer ball was invented by Charles Goodyear in 1855. It had rubber panels and looked similar to today's volleyballs.

SOCCER BALL FROM 1930

Modern companies are still trying to improve the soccer ball. They've used different materials and panel shapes. Some are experimenting with putting a camera inside the ball!

MODERN SOCCER BALL

Midfielders get their name from the part of the field they play most on—the middle of the field. They are often the most fit players on the team because they must help both the offense and defense.

DID YOU KNOW?

Soccer players run far more than football or baseball players.

In **professional** soccer games, players run back and forth on fields that are at least 110 yards (101 m) long and 70 yards (64 m) wide. Many players run about 7 miles (11.3 km) during a game. Midfielders have been known to run more than 9 miles (14.5 km) in a game!

THE RULES OF THE GAME

DID YOU KNOW?

The clock never stops ticking during a soccer match.

A soccer game is 90 minutes long, with two 45-minute halves. If **injuries** occur or the ball goes out of play, an official keeps track of the time that is lost. Minutes are added on to the end of each half. This is called stoppage or injury time.

Soccer officials can add time to a half if one team wastes time or for any other reason they decide. Stoppage time is usually between 1 and 4 extra minutes.

When a ball goes out of bounds, a player is allowed to pick it up and use both hands to throw the ball back into play.

DID YOU KNOW?

Goalkeepers, also called keepers, are the only players who can touch the ball with their hands while on the field.

Keepers can only touch the ball with their hands inside their own 40-yard (36.6 m) box. Teammates can only use their head to pass back to a keeper. If teammates pass to a keeper with their feet, keepers also have to use their feet!

DID YOU KNOW?

Soccer officials didn't use color-coded cards until 1970.

During the 1970 Word Cup, English **referee** Ken Alston became the first official to use color-coded **foul** cards. Referees raised the card in the air, then wrote the name of the player carded on the back to keep track of the fouls.

A yellow card is a warning, but a red card means a player has to leave the game! A red card can also result in a player being banned for a number of games.

YELLOW AND RED

WHAT DO THEY MEAN?

YELLOW CARD

BEING A BAD SPORT
BAD LANGUAGE
ROUGH PLAY
WASTING TIME
LEAVING THE FIELD WITHOUT PERMISSION
NOT LISTENING TO AN OFFICIAL

RED CARD

TWO YELLOW CARDS
RECKLESS, OR DANGEROUS, PLAY
FIGHTING
SWEARING AND SPITTING
USE OF HANDS TO STOP A SCORING CHANCE IN THE GOALIE BOX

THE WORLD'S GAME

DID YOU KNOW?

The soccer capital of the world is Zurich, Switzerland.

The Fédération Internationale de Football Association (FIFA) was formed in 1904. It was founded in Paris, France, but later moved its headquarters to Zurich, Switzerland. FIFA sets the rules for soccer around the world.

FIFA was originally made up of 7 European countries. Today, it includes 211 teams worldwide.

An English team can play in the Premier League and also compete for an association's trophy, like UEFA's (Union of European Football Associations) Champions League.

DID YOU KNOW?

Soccer clubs can play for many different trophies.

Professional soccer teams play in a domestic league, which is based in a country like England, Brazil, or the United States. Different associations also hold tournaments throughout the season. When teams win their domestic league and their top association trophy in one season, it's called a "double"!

GOLD!

DID YOU KNOW?

Soccer players love playing for gold.

Many of the top prizes in soccer are gold. Both the men's and women's World Cup trophies are golden prizes given to the winner of the international tournament. A Golden Boot is often given to the top goal scorer in tournaments and leagues.

Every year, the best men's soccer player in the world is given the Ballon d'Or, French for "golden ball." Lionel Messi of Argentina has won the most Ballon d'Or trophies with eight.

SOCCER'S GOLDEN GOALS

OLYMPIC GOLD MEDAL
Olympic Games champion

BALLON D'OR
top player of the year

WORLD CUP TROPHY
World Cup champion

BRITISH PREMIER LEAGUE TROPHY
Premier League champion

GOLDEN BOOT
top goal scorer of a World Cup tournament

WOMEN'S WORLD CUP TROPHY
Women's World Cup champion

U.S. SOCCER

DID YOU KNOW?

All Major League Soccer (MLS) teams are owned by MLS!

No person or group owns a Major League Soccer (MLS) team. Owners invest in, or put money into, the league itself and are given a stake in a team. Some owners actually have stakes in multiple teams!

MSL was founded in 1993. As of 2025, the league has 27 U.S. teams and 3 Canadian teams. The LA Galaxy has won the most MSL titles with 6.

Donovan has helped win 6 MSL titles. The MLS most valuable player award is now named after him!

DID YOU KNOW?

Landon Donovan is widely considered the best American player ever.

Donovan played forward with the San Jose Earthquake and LA Galaxy between 2001 and 2014. He finished his career with 144 goals and 136 assists (which is a league record). He also has 57 goals playing the U.S. National Team.

TRADES AND LOANS

DID YOU KNOW?

In many professional sports leagues, players are traded from one team to another. However, in the MLS, players are sold to other teams.

When one club wants a player owned by another team, they pay a transfer fee. The rights to the player move to the new team, and the player switches clubs. The player also signs a new contract with the new team.

Getting a new player can cost huge amounts of money. When a small club sells a player to a large club, it can often fund the small club's entire budget for a season!

DID YOU KNOW?

Teams can also loan players to other teams!

In 2010 and 2012, the LA Galaxy loaned Landon Donovan to the English club Everton.

Loaned players are still under contract with their first club, but play for a different team. Some players are loaned to get more playing time at a smaller club. Others are loaned because a team doesn't want the player anymore.

MEMORABLE MOMENTS

DID YOU KNOW?

One of the greatest goals of all time should not have been a goal.

In the 1986 World Cup, Argentina's Diego Maradona scored a goal with his raised left hand! The goal counted and earned Maradona the nickname "Hand of God." Five minutes later, Maradona ran by English players to score what is now called the "Goal of the Century." Argentina beat England, 2–1.

Maradona's second goal was a 60-yard (55 m) sprint through five British players! It's thought to be one of the greatest goals of all time.

Two of the greatest all-time players, Lionel Messi (Barcelona) and Christiano Ronaldo (Real Madrid), met often during El Clásico matches. Messi has the most El Clásico goals in history with 26. Ronaldo shares second place with another player with 18 goals.

DID YOU KNOW?

One of the biggest matches in soccer is known as "El Clásico."

El Clásico is any match between Real Madrid and FC Barcelona, two **rival** Spanish clubs that play in the top Spanish league, La Liga. Soccer fans around the world tune in any time these two teams meet on the pitch.

U.S. WOMEN'S SOCCER

DID YOU KNOW?

The United States has won the most Women's World Cups.

The first Women's World Cup was held in 1991. The United States won the first tournament, beating Norway, 2–1. It also beat China in 1999 and Japan in 2015. In 2019, the U.S. women's team beat the Netherlands 2–0 for a fourth World Cup title.

Abby Wambach has scored the most World Cup goals for the U.S. women's team with 14. In fact, Wambach holds the record for most international goals with 184!

The United States scored four goals in 16 minutes during their 5-2 win against Japan. They only needed Lloyd's three!

DID YOU KNOW?

Carli Lloyd scored a hat trick during a Women's World Cup Final!

Lloyd scored the first hat trick (3 goals in one game) in Women's World Cup Finals history. Her first three shots on goal in the 2015 Women's World Cup Final were goals! Lloyd scored in the third minute, the sixth minute, and the 16 minute.

BEAUTIFUL GAME

The sport of soccer is often called the "beautiful game," a term popularized by one of soccer's greatest players ever—Pelé. Talented players spread out all over the world make for lots of great soccer matches. There's always a new team to learn about or great new players to watch. Some of them might even join your favorite club.

The more you watch and play soccer, the more fun facts you'll learn about this great sport. Maybe you'll watch your favorite team win the double. Or, maybe you'll get to play in the World Cup Final one day!

Edson Arantes do Nascimento—or Pelé as he was known—played professional soccer from 1956 to 1977. He was so good that some of his records still stand to this day!

GLOSSARY

association: A group with similar interests.

bladder: An organ of the body that can stretch and holds fluids.

budget: A planned amount of money available for a purpose.

champion: Having to do with the winner of a contest or tournament.

foul: An act that breaks a rule.

injury: Hurt or loss.

professional: Having to do with something people do for a living.

slang: A nonstandard word used to refer to something.

referee: Someone who judges a game to make it fair.

rival: One of two groups that compete against each other often.

tournament: A contest of skill played by many different teams.

valuable: Important.

FOR MORE INFORMATION

BOOKS

Krenn, Cara. *Best Women's Soccer Players.* Minneapolis, MN: Lerner Publications, 2025.

Mugford, Simon. *Soccer Stories: My World Cup Heroes.* London, UK: Welbeck Children's Books, 2025.

WEBSITES

Fédération Internationale de Football Association
fifa.com
Learn more about international soccer on the official FIFA site.

Major League Soccer
mlssoccer.com
Find out more about your favorite U.S. teams at the official site of Major League Soccer.

Premier League Soccer
premierleague.com
Learn more about England's best teams on the official BPL site.

Publisher's note to educators and parents: Our editors have carefully reviewed these websites to ensure that they are suitable for students. Many websites change frequently, however, and we cannot guarantee that a site's future contents will continue to meet our high standards of quality and educational value. Be advised that students should be closely supervised whenever they access the internet.

INDEX